The Same Water

Wesleyan New Poets

The Same Water

Poems by
Joan Murray

Wesleyan University Press
Middletown, Connecticut

Some of these poems originally appeared in *The Hudson Review*, *Ms.*, *The Ontario Review*, *The Paris Review*, and *Prairie Schooner.* "The Bloody Show" appeared in a chapbook.

The first epigraph on page vi is from the water riddle by Aldhelm, Abbot of Malmesbury, and is translated from his Latin by the author.

The author is grateful to the New York State CAPS Program, the New York State Council on the Arts, the New York Foundation for the Arts, and the National Endowment for the Arts for the fellowships and grants that supported the work in this collection.

All inquiries and permissions requests should be addressed to the Publisher, Wesleyan University Press, 110 Mt. Vernon Street, Middletown, Connecticut 06457

LIBRARY OF CONGRESS CATALOGING-IN-PUBLICATION DATA

Murray, Joan.
  The same water / Joan Murray. – 1st ed.
    p.   cm. – (Wesleyan new poets)
  ISBN 0–8195–1183–8   ISBN 0–8195–2181–7
  I. Title. II. Series.
  PS3563.U7694S2 1990
  811'.54–dc20   89–33954
                        CIP

Manufactured in the United States of America

First Edition

Contents

Who wouldn't be struck by the spectacle
    of my fate:
I'll be carrying with force a thousand
    forest oaks,
But then the thinnest needle breaks all
    my bearing.

—7th Century Riddle

"Can you row?" the Sheep asked,
handing her a pair of knitting-needles. . . .

—*Through the Looking Glass*

The Same Water

Coming of Age on the Harlem

for Kathy

1

My father would tie a life jacket
to a length of seaworn rope and dangle me
off the dock of the Harlem Boat Club float.
A strange baptism.
Down, down into the mad rushing river,
worm on a hook, a girl of six or seven,
I am let loose among water rats, made sister
to half-filled soda cans floating
vertically home from a picnic, and to condoms
that look like mama doll socks
in the unopened infant eye.
What man would toss his child to that swill?
He who can swim across the river,
whose arms churn a feud with the current.
He thinks he can hold me from any maelstrom.
Safe on the dock, I watch my father
float on his back, from the Bronx
to Manhattan and back again.

2

Between the river edge and river park,
the New York Central tracks could fry a child.
How lucky to have this father with
long, strong arms to whisk me over
the wooden-hooded, menacing third rail.
Can you remember when you reached your father's waist
and he told you of the serpent track where
only birds could land in safety?
But one day my father takes me home a different way:
up the wooden bridge above the tracks
where huge phallic shapes have been burned in black
along its walls. Don't look. Don't look.
That sight will fry you up like Semele.
Now my strong father, my never ruffled father

3

pulls me roughly over the wooden planks.
His dark face reddened tells of great,
unspoken danger. When we reach the street,
he makes me promise never to come this way again,
never to go to the river shore without him.
Over my shoulder I form an opposite determination.

3

The Harlem Boat Club is the man place.
My father slips down twice a week to shower,
on weekends plays a sweaty game
of four-wall ball. Outside in the garden,
I wander six years old among lilies
of the valley, Queen Anne's lace,
the shoreline irises and great climbing rose
that began as someone's potted plant.
Elmer, the muscular black cat,
drags a water rat to the front door. I follow inside
to the boat room, run my hand along
the lean flanks of polished rowing sculls,
then up the stairway, pause at the wooden roster,
the names with gold stars dead in some war.
Then the sweat smell of the lockers,
the place where they held a party
to welcome the Beatty brothers home from Korea.
Off to the side, three men stand
naked in the steamy, tiled shower.
Quiet, I sit down on a bench
beside a girl my own age, who has also come
to pretend she doesn't notice.

4

Still my close, though distant, friend,
who sat with me in the men's locker room,
whose father had a strong right arm for handball,
whose mother and mine, embarrassed

in their forties, had pregnancies,
who accompanied me through puberty
up and down the Harlem shore,
Kathy, in your Brahmin home in Brooklyn,
you say you want to rid your sleep of those
dirty years along the river. But stop for a moment,
stop trying to make the river pass genteelly,
for there'll be no weaning from those waters.
Instead come back with me and watch
the sun glint off the rippling surface,
bearing the shore-hugging flow of turds and
condoms north to the Hudson.
You conjectured it all came from cabin cruisers
on some far-off glory ocean.
Kathy, would you have even looked
if you had known it came from humble tenements
on our Highbridge hill?
Could that one reflection
have darkened all your plans to sail?

    5

"Mirror, Mirror"
was the name you gave him
a dexterous man with a pocket mirror
who could catch the Sunday-morning sun
and flash it on our untouched child bodies.
Snow White gone haywire, Rapunzel in reverse:
"Mirror, Mirror!"
we shouted from the bridge height,
and he below us in the river park would
hold his instrument to the sky like
a sextant and calculate his grotesque angles.
Then we'd race down the ramp
just beyond his unknown reach and dive
behind the safety of a tree.
Oh God! Oh God! the heavy breathing,

ours, his, the fear, the vague desire
that was always escaped in time to
run home at one for Sunday dinner and meet our
unsuspecting fathers coming home from mass.

6

Just before ten, just before your father's curfew,
you can station yourself on the highway bridge, where
it joins the ramp from the river park,
to see the couples rise up on the evening tide:
the sooty venuses with dirty hand marks
on white and fondled blouses, and
their boyfriends swaggering in teenage jeans.
You laugh, and send your first awakening lust
to follow them back to the neighborhood
where someday all will notice that you've grown.
And small children will stand on bridges
to flank your path
as you make your debut entry
to the nightly river-park cotillion, on the arm
of some lanky boy with a dangling black curl,
and the cleanest, oh the cleanest hands.

7

It's the boys with sprouts of pubic hair
who have the manliness to strip and jump
while tourists on the Circle Line around
Manhattan watch with Brownie cameras.
Bright-faced fathers and mothers, pointing out
the river life to their children.
They look for street kids in straw hats,
the Tom Sawyers and Huck Finns of the Harlem,
but only get an upraised finger.
Behind the nude boys who perch on river rocks
and invite the sun to their members,
a dozen girls, in tight black shorts and

ponytails, keep a coy but glancing distance.
And behind them all, a white-haired voyeur
drops his pants to masturbate.
The eyes of the Circle Line sail upriver, still
hopeful that Becky Thatcher in eyelet bloomers
will wave a hanky from the shore.

8

In Undercliff Park, below Washington Bridge,
I play stretch and toe-knee-chest-nut with
my father's pocketed army knife.
A dangerous age. Threats are cutting through the air:
the flailing depantsings, the groping bra quests for
a wad of cotton or a nylon stocking.
A dangerous age, with the deadly fear
of being found a child.
To relieve it one day, we hang a tire in a tree and
swing in packs out over the cliff edge,
until the boy beside me loses grip, and lies
below, as quiet as an infant in a lullaby.
Weeks later, we visit him at home, sign his casts
and giggle at his immature pajamas.
He lifts his mattress to show
an arsenal of thirty knives and ice picks,
and lets each girl pick a pocket lighter
shoplifted from Woolworth's.

9

Hung by my hands above water,
I am dangled by boys from the ledge
of the Washington Bridge abutment.
Twelve years old, twelve feet from the surface,
I do not trust boys, but love their giddy danger
like a windflaw teasing with a sail.
And while we dangle, the boys hurl rocks
at the river, waiting for the splash that will leap

up to our blouses and clutch the outlines
of our forming breasts.
Soaked through, we climb the naked limbs
of a shore tree and sprawl in the afternoon sun.
Above, a boy hovers in the branches,
reaches for my hand a moment and is gone,
leaving something growing in me
that holds me separate from my friends
as we walk together to our fathers' houses,
wearing our secret scent of the river.

10

My husband no more "swims b.a."
I can no longer picture his shadow
rippling across the sidewalks to the Harlem.
A swaggering, older boy, once unattainable.
Now at night I cradle his black hair
to my breast and we share the river's secrets:
My splashing joyride pickup with three strange boys
in a motorboat. His first hesitating touch
of Dodie, the hillbilly girl on the fourteen steps
below Macombs Dam Bridge.
The tales of all those years I was not permitted
at the Harlem, unless my father stood beside me,
gathering me into his safe garden. All those years
I learned the route to avoid his path.
Now I retrace it in the dark, step by step, till
again I watch the Harlem Boat Club burn, and see
the steps plucked from the river bridge
where no child can again take the path
that leads me nightly to this good bed.
Kathy, did we escape our fathers?
Or did they plan our turns and detours
just carefully enough to lead us here?

The Unmolested Child

They will not let me off till I go with them, respond to them,
And discorrupt them, and charge them full with the charge of the soul.

Prelude

Waiting on the stairs of the Mizpah Missionary Home on
Summit Avenue, the children of apostles played with
neighborhood kids and sometimes spread the gospel, warming
up for the prodigious conversions on another continent.
Prior to departure, one boy had brought a hand generator,
and we would all connect, hold the metal railing of
the steps, a human chain out to the light pole, to test
our conductivity and our resistance.
He'd wind the rotor, send out waves of electricity,
jolt us and knock us down like the Easter-morning soldiers.
And quieter, inside, his parents gave us
threads to wind around two fingers. Easy to break
a few encirclings. But impossible,
the repeated bindings. A lesson on bad habits,
still retained from Sundays with the Good Samaritan
and the even better candy in our hands.

And each six weeks the sermon changed,
the family was replaced. There was the girl,
for instance, who made disciples of the boys. Who taught
a lesson to us girls on envy. She used her breasts,
pale and long. She lay with Huey Lally in the sun.
She had probably seen it done in Africa. A most simple
habit and routine. But seeing them lying in that state
in the public river park, we the uninitiate and
unredeemed, were doubly shocked.
The boys strained their necks from the rock outcrop
we called "the Alamo" which overlooked the Harlem River.
The sun was strong that summer. There was no
lightning bolt to get her. Six weeks we went ignored.

After she had gone, Huey got his cough.
He went insulted up and down our neighborhood.

9

We called him "Marbles." His voice had taken on
a sound like grinding glass. It was puberty,
we thought, this deepening that had come on with shaving.
We made him pay though she had brought it on, of course.
But then it progressed to where we couldn't call it off,
to where he showed me from his bed, the new
air rifle from his father, his plans for it as hollow
as his eyes. Before I left he signed
my eighth-grade autograph book: "Ashes to ashes,
dust to dust." The next month he was dead.

And there it was, unmistakable, the connecting thread
from God who frowns on adolescent lust, who mistook
a desecration of his maiden, who
sent that boy a bolt we never wished him.
Not Nola Diaz and Kathy Smyth, who loved him. Not I,
so crushed I wrote his mother something now forgotten,
that made her beg me to drop by,
to tell all the things she didn't know about him,
to keep him alive, she said.

I

On a curbstone above a sewer I sit with my brother
while the sun gathers back its light, for
a moment intensifies, then retracts from our extending
shadows and climbs down behind the Harlem River.
Until it's gone, we'll watch the older boys contend
with sawed-off broomsticks and "spauldeens."
Where Woodycrest intersects our street, each base is
a corner sewer. The center manhole,
the unelevated pitcher's mound. They let us sit on
third. The ball is soft and no one will get hurt.

Then from behind us, like the sudden angel
whose low reconnaissance spots the children
on the cliff, or on the slim bridge above the rapids,
he appears, the artistic nursery scene: two periled
children and the angel intervenes to save, we all
presumed, and not to push. But notice his finger.
How willfully it points at me. The same gesture which,
with matured iconology, we'll recognize in those great
depictions of unsettling authority: where it
points the lounging Adam from the comfort of
his loam. Points the tender Mary from her tranquil
broom and dust. Points the tender boy to man artillery.
I want you, says your uncle. His gesture
clearly to distrust, but I was six, and schooled toward
the comfort of strangers. And here a strange man
needing, that night, to get engaged. A man who in
a nearby basement had lost "a blue diamond ring"
and asked me if I'd help him find it.

No matter the huddling girl on the front stoop
as he took me to the alley of my building. No matter
her plea, "Don't go with him." How matter-of-factly
he took my hand and told me, "Don't be afraid."

I was no coward: I watched stickball.
She lived around the corner, played with dolls.
My brother tagged along. But that was useless.
The stranger set his hopes on me. He squeezed
my hand, exercised his authority, gave directions
to my brother to search the yard where a cracked
couch and matching chair waited for the junkman's truck.

And I went with him. Into the second basement,
past the dark storeroom that held my grandmother's
bridal bed with pineapples on its posts,
past where the dumbwaiters waited in their walls,
to where the boiler room was darker. And there
he stood before me, positioning me, eliciting a
promise of secrecy. I still was calm. But then
an actual angel came. I grew afraid and ran.
Not knowing why. Up to my apartment
terrified, unable to explain, except, "There was a man."
My father and my uncle Marty raced down the
stairs, understanding that danger I could not describe.

Three weeks I had to stay inside. Then it was the police
in a car with lights and all, that took my brother and me
to the station. And there was their suspect
on the stoop of the 44th precinct, between four men and
the tall globes of justice that still face the river.
Identification was expected.
I wore my newest sundress with alphabet letters,
and was sure of almost twenty-six. They said he had
confessed. But his face seemed tanner, his hair
seemed longer. It wasn't him, I said.
My brother, undecided, sided with me. We were told
the other girl had recognized him: She, the one who
played with dolls. That night they had to let him go.

I was then, what I took for, a celebrity.
And dangerously took my friends to see the refreshment
stand his family ran under the shuttle El near
Macombs Dam Park, just north of Yankee Stadium.
He had a history of taking small girls in the dark
and doing what I didn't know. That thing
that enraged my father so, that made my mother
whisper over the one washer in the basement laundry room.
That thing I'm sure that huddling girl
could have told. But I never saw her.
The more reliable witness, who moved away that summer.

II

Tie to tie I walk the tunnel
from its mouth on the Harlem River where we'd
broken in, to Anderson Avenue on the other
side of the neighborhood, passing under my father's
couch as he naps between his jobs at the center of
One Hundred Sixty-second Street where, deep below,
the newly abandoned IRT tunnel bends into its darkest,
and I go: an assignation.
I spare him the expense of worry. Let him sleep
above me like the bearded God who gets
winded at our games.
I will emerge whole from beneath gas lines and
sewage pipes, and will boost myself up from the track
to the open-air platform, and there remember waiting once
early in the morning with my mother
and seeing the elongate spokes of the rounded iron
fence, I took it for an emblem of the sun.
Fierce and glorious. I did not apprehend
it stood against intrusion. I had taken
it as art, meaningful and useless, at an age
when I still knelt on subways and stared
into that dark and was good at taking
the occasional flicker in.

Now on the platform, corrected by
that fence, I regard it as a barrier, perceive
some loss of innocence. I wait here for a boy,
thirteen like me, sent down the eastbound track
while I walked down the west.
Pyramus and Thisbe in our jeans, we went, though,
of course, we'd never heard such things.
And now I could not hear his footfalls,
though he must have been there, just to my left.

Only the seepage water running down the walls,
the recurrent hum of hotboxes lying
in the tracks, charged still with electricity,
I was careful to step over.
A quarter way I went, looking back at what
was light. And the next quarter, at the hardly light
dying into the solid dark of the tunnel's bend,
and there the absolute aloneness magnified.
Only the ties counted out loud with sneaker feet kept
my heart intact. Oh how it beat until that first
barely and doubted light was real and finally there.

And I arrived too frightened to entertain desires
that my friends back on the Harlem side would be
imagining for me in this tunnel of love, of our
breakings and enterings, where I realized
there was no one else but me.
Not once did I fear for him or picture how he might
have touched something dangerous, forbidden, how he'd
been terribly burned, or how, halfway turned,
a loss of will. I knew I was abandoned: I was being
joked at. Or at least rejected. The rules were
broken. The board bumped, its pieces strewn, and I
marooned at the far end of a tunnel where he would not
come, I knew. And yet I stayed there much too long,
rummaging my head for some prescription gleaned from
teenage comic books. But there was no reference yet
to the old tunnel, where she always waits
for his arrival. The game was over early. The winter
sun soon gone from the barricaded station.
And no way back but to take that dark again.

III

It was Kathy Shackel who was caught
in the *Daily News* with a tissue at her nose.
Tomorrow she'd be explaining she simply had
a cold, but the photographer had waited for some
symbol while we stood so stoically on the steps
and the summoned baritone and tenor wove
those woeful Latins in the loft.
It was Roseanne Breen, whom we'd least expected
to be at the center of such a scene.
Roseanne Breen, only eleven, her integrity so
intact that she never played at the forbidden river
where our parents would not let us go.
Never posed there in *her* bathing suit
for the man who claimed he'd come from
Confidential Magazine:
That year we had thought we'd all be famous,
and so trustingly, we thumbed those seamy
pages and grew impatient and confused as we
waited to appear. Then one of us concluded:
we had been used. Maybe we had known it
since that day we so eagerly made
fools of ourselves, smiled and moved
the way he told us, displayed our naivete.

And now it was Kathy Shackel in the centerfold
and Margie Daniels quoted on page three for
what her mother had seen while Margie was
with me at the river, and we were endangered
only by the current, the cliff and tracks.
Coming home with sacks of groceries that afternoon,
Mrs. Daniels noticed a stain on the mosaic tiles near
the stairs, and found beneath them, a naked child
so stabbed and bloody it could not
be recognized. She thought it was her own.

What could our parents say? We who had
disobeyed, who had gone out where all their restrictions,
all their predictions of jeopardy applied,
instead were safe. And she who had dutifully stayed home
to do her homework was now inside
the box coming footfirst down the steps.
The next-door neighbor had confessed. He, the father
of two small girls, who were not there that afternoon
he made an abattoir of their living room.
But he never had entered her, he argued. Never had
penetrated her, he said. So Roseanne Breen, who was
so featured in the *Daily News* that none of us
forgets, who was eleven when we saw her last,
is unmolested still.

IV

Complacencies of our Saturday afternoons,
we'd drop beneath the landing of the footbridge
where it pauses on a retaining wall between its
crossings of the Deegan highway and the Central
tracks that ran along the Harlem River.
And there, congenial on a shelf of concrete where
a slip would have had us on those tracks,
we sat, prolonging conversation with conventional
slang. Or inventing insults. I was good at that.
And maybe someone passed a can of any beer for all
our unrefined distaste. Boys spat. Girls combed their
hair. The Camels and the Lucky Strikes got shared.
Every gesture, every posture was arranged,
the orchestrations for our fourteen years.

And then from that narrow line, Billy MacDonald,
loud, tall and a little overweight, would rise, begin
to pace, then haul himself onto the bridge
and we would follow, to watch for Frieda.
Frieda, who would soon crown the steps, her breasts
heaving beneath her sad and European face, her
alien slacks too tight above dismal oxford shoes.
A girl we others would usually torment, but now
we were silent, watching gravely the immensity
of her descent, her downcast eyes, her
hurried intent to run our gauntlet unabused.

And he, too, would say nothing to her. Act almost
as if he didn't know her. Precede her clumsily
over the steel railings. Not take her hand.
Not help her jump from the concrete abutment
to the slope that led to the shuttle tunnel entrance.
Not hold back the flap of metal curtain
we had cut. Not turn to see if she had
squeezed successfully through the iron fence we'd bent.

And yet how willingly she went, for what that unlikely
boy could activate below the tapped-out change booth
in the eerie airless room where we'd found
a welded crate still filled with workmen's tools.
For some movie we had seen, we named it "Kali's Tomb."

We could, of course, picture, despite relative
inexperience, what was exchanged there: what passed
between lips and hands, what leaned against
the wall, what was built and what was spent.
But there was something more. And we were ignorant.
When she'd come out alone (he'd come out later),
we would stare, feel smaller in the presence
of what she'd got in there, now emergent from
that sibylline cave with all that wisdom so distending
it raised her head, her shoulders, as she rose
from the river on her shell, self-absorbed and
unaware of us. With all that interior
knowledge. All that conviction she was loved.

V

An unprecedented vantage. From here a child could scan all
the architectonics of the Harlem: the disjunct perspective
of buildings not yet burned, and down to her left,
Yankee Stadium. And the Polo Grounds
still standing to her right, and, closer,
the Wilson Tower, where neighbor wives
bring to light *The Reader's Guide to Periodical Literature*
and still are home by five. And the meat
loafs in its pan. And each thing finds its place.
It is rare at that height, where she is transfigured like
Christ in space, on "a pinnacle of the temple" or the
"exceeding high mountain" where he was bribed with all
the kingdoms of the world, unlike this girl who's come
for a candy on a stick and the promise of a dime.

Both will do what's expected.
The world will sigh and hurl on as planned.
When Lenny Freitag phones to say what's turned up
on the concrete canopy above the Projects' door
below seventeen floors, it won't be Christ,
and I'll reflect on Michael Maydie's eyes,
pointed out to me outside the A&P, just before the
bus doors closed. Visibly insane, only eleven, did
it take another child to know?

And I will redefine a high view, reshape at ten
the topography of the Harlem to include the incomprehensible
need to simply kill someone, and the insubstantial
cohesion of the body, and the rotten
luck of election. And we will say how fine
she looks, a child of six with her hair
so fashionably curled, her left cheek hardly
broken. Her sister Rita who sits next to me in class, by
contrast, will be paler, thin. Haggard by graduation.
The other sister will grow fat, her name forgotten.

But held aloft now, over the ledge, Kathy Hagman
can see at once all the bridges of our Harlem, the lengths
we all have crossed: the Washington, Third Avenue and
Macombs Dam. The IRT shuttle bridge, soon left open,
the highway footbridge, and the older river one
with its aqueduct and arches that will one day appear so
famously in our high-school Latin books, on whose
span the widowed Poe once walked, waving to demons in
the tide, and thought to make that walk his last.
But he turned instead through farmers' fields, across
the Bronx to the straw-stuffed bed we looked at once,
and wrote a consolation, an explanation for
all these things: the garbled lamentation, "Ulalume."
So let's be off to rave and run our circles, to clean and
put away the pans, to welcome to our burned-out shelters,
the pending, black ball that makes room for others,
to be gone before she lands.

The Bloody Show

At nineteen the birth is early.
The waters break before dark.

                      Tomorrow morning,
the doctor says by phone.
My mother makes her pilgrimage
    fearing I will not complete this thing
without her,
            though our women have a history
of birth.

The morning cannot wait, she says.
The bloody show has come.
                Reluctant,
she leaves me to a cabbie who
drives, for no reason, to the West Side Highway.
Like Bethlehem, the rooms are full.
And the bloody show insists
                it will be now.

But the doctor has not come. The birth
may not proceed.
         I am stored away, denied
the room to move this child from me.
A nurse comes, listens to the secrets
of the fetal heart,
         draws an x on my abdomen,
does not return.

I count the squares of the tiled walls, grip
the pipes and valves
          behind my head,
squeeze the sides of the narrow table.
Far down the hall a woman screams.
              Another language
but I know her meaning.
This child cannot wait. It comes, the body

taking over.
     Something breaks. A rush
of blood
at the doctor's entry.

Someone clean this mess, he shouts.
He makes no greeting.
I am lifted to a stretcher,
wheeled to delivery, halfway through
         the birth
and then the ether.

Now
  week after week
       my breasts
drop milk. The doctor will not stop it.
  My mother tells what she never told
about this doctor
      who came too late
ten years before to deliver her son.
She watched a nurse take the child
  through a haze of ether.
       They told her she was wrong.

In three weeks my daughter Kristin
has died from her broken heart.
       A freak
of nature, says the doctor. There will
be others.
    The next week I phone to ask him
to prescribe some exercise.
      Just push the carriage, he says.

Madonna vs. Child

for my son Jim

I

I expect no man to understand.
The womb has so complicated everything.
        Someday in a business suit
you may stop at lunchtime and
        picture yourself tucked up in
the broody gloom of the ovary and stirred one night
by a quick ejaculation.
        It's embarrassing. At best, confusing.
More comfortable, a conception in a glass
or stainless steel, sanitized and
sealed, no cleaving bonds.
        But flesh will not forget its
groaning, momentary, pinioned breach of
freedom as you came,
    your greasy, bloody head intruding
in the mirror where there had been nothing.
And the moment extends itself:
        forever pinioned
beneath a thing that emerged
raw and weighty as a batch of clay, and
    trailing that leeching cord.
How ugly we both were, battered and exhausted
as something forced us into those complicated
        and absurd postures
and insisted that all this be done.
I expect no man will fully understand.
    I won't ask more of you.
None of this was my design. I
would have been glad to find you dropped among
the split wood of the fireplace
and hear the wings rushing away,
the voiceless clatter of the unburdened bird
        drifting through the downdraft.

II

And now the balance is undone,
    the calm keel jostled by your coming.
Our wills wrestle above the crib, and you,
squat stowaway, must win.
Overpowering with frailty, your
                            trivial fingers flare out
their distress, your lungs raise up
a tyrant SOS.
Once I could have stood aloof
    like a watcher on some isolated shore, amused at
the excesses of a courting sandpiper's
                          ruffled-up display.
But your long conspiracy with nature is too shrewd:
I am at your will.
I offer my breast to you, as I would to no other
                              stranger.
You
    will survive.
Take your place before me in this boat where
I once sat, assured of my own skin.
Your weight pitches the balance I had managed to maintain.
        In the end, I know it is I
who must go over.

III

How easy it will be to say this
                once it's said.
It will pale the pinks and blues of nurseries,
the maternity gowns with their flowery collars, hanging
    in the attics, the paper cards with everyone's
                congratulations, bundled up in rubber bands.
Look instead at the ties which we must
wear forever now, clownish
as a pair of actors dressed
        in schoolboy clothes, for the bond still holds us
to who we were on that erupting morning,
    and fixes us, madonna and child, by the flesh.
Look at our other postures, each one contrived
dissoluble, changing daily, hourly:
a head bowed in disappointment, a shoulder
slouched in disregard, a finger flying out with
                accusation, a foot drumming
                                its impatience.
Each pose collapses
beneath the weight of our anatomy:
                                of where you began
before you became.
If you think that imposes too much on you,
understand it is impossible for either one of
    us to wriggle free.
Child, you are my future. I am your history.

The Precarious Nest

This summer I am less affected by Darwin
and the ice-action and organic production
of the Southern Hemisphere,
                    or by his expedition
up the Santa Cruz where he saw streams of stones, fires
        made of bones,
                    and shot a condor.
    or even by his exploration of Tierra del Fuego where
in winter hunger, men ate their mothers
                    and kept their dogs.

I am drawn more this morning to Gilbert White
making a treatise of the harvest mouse
in his own garden,
                    or becoming expert in the swallows
he flushed from the banks along his daily walk
        in Selborne.

And I am positively at home today, early as it is, with
        John Ray, nine years observing the plants
that grew around his own door in Cambridge,
    and becoming a father, finally at fifty-seven,
coming back to a cottage in Black Notley
            and sending out his four young daughters
to collect caterpillars and butterflies
                    for him to classify.

Here on my own narrow sun porch with its thirteen-dozen
panes of old imperfect glass, I have been
making sense of this universe.

Already this morning I have observed a robin
springing across the asphalt shingles of the garage roof,
                pausing to listen, impossibly
for worms.
And the cat
        hardly visible in the rose hedge.

And through these same panes I've watched
Ann Williams under the birch tree with her new
husband's shirt,
  managing to thread a needle in the wind.

    And Carol Wright cutting down the privet hedge
that would not leaf after the cold winter
and her divorce.

Daily I looked for the corpse of
a small starling to dry and flatten so the wind could
take it off the sloped porch
        beneath the bedroom window.
           But first
a heavy rain.

And I saw where, from the same precarious nest
built in the valley below the gable-dormer eave,
another hatchling,
    naked and all head,
had toppled, bounced and landed in the uncut grass.
    It stayed alive all night
in a box of straw outside the attic window.

But there are four, maybe even six,
unmarked eggs in a starling's nest.

Here I have been waked by the distressed
yelping of the Campbell's black dog, and
stuck on its back, caught in the act,
      the Bachs' black dog.
  Before sunup Saturday, and the Bachs' lights
on all night for the sabbath.
      Then a neighbor running with a hose.

I now know that bees doze intoxicated
under the lime tree at the corner.
          And turning the other corner one evening
stung in the neck by a honeybee
                              coming from nowhere
and so unreasonable.

I have proof now that a new cat escaping down a
vine through a broken upstairs screen,
          returning that night, afraid, will cling
midway up the insubstantial strand
                    even if the back door is wide open for her.

My hands are the ones that steady the ladder.
My husband fears height.

Squirrels leap unhesitatingly from wire to wire,
          then to the shed dormer, the garage roof.
They understand foreplay.
                              They enjoy their tails.

John Putnam, though a naval commander,
sings a sweet high formless aria when he
walks the old collie now before bedtime.
          My husband wonders if he's drinking.

Crows do not sing *down a down*.
They make a harsh din, and it's easy to think
          they see trouble coming.
But I believe they mean no harm.

                    The fierce territoriality
of our courting cardinal.
          And yet his amiable song.

The tomato vines are six feet high now, strung on
    electrical conduit pipes.
The zucchinis, gigantic,
      pregnant, yet phallic,
  hang over into the driveway.
        We park the car on the street.

The cardinals built in the honeysuckle
   before the new cat.
The new cat has mastered its climbing.
Objectivity is an aim of the natural scientist.

From the sun porch by moonlight, looking west
I can see, on *their* sun porch,
      the Williams' brace
of exercise bikes, riderless all night.
And to the east, Carol Wright's facing the dark tv
with its solitary wheel.

Soon Nathan Bach, framed in the high shadeless
   window, will be davening in his shawl.
His search for meaning, like my own, goes on,
not leading to his loss of freedom,
or anything else's.

Whatever we prayed to once
is there outside the porch panes, still
      answering or ignoring our prayers.

There is always some weed that the garden loves.

The Grotte des Infants

1

Seventeen years and again the wet sheet,
a stain from something given way.
    A thing had whimpered somewhere in that
room. My legs bound to metal stirrups,
I could not see, and there was no one
to tell me, but called your name and knew
which name to use.

Was it the emptiness I was in that moment,
strapped open in communion with the wide, dark
gapes between the stars. Did I hope
by that calling to spare you what
        few things I could: the futile
rib, the womb of oceans drained by each moon,
the lacteal sacs borne all those years
                for that whimpering.

I was the first to say your name. The first
to ask you to keep silent.

2

After the first emergence. Brought back together
again. Again. The blood to the sheet.
    A nail in your sole. The hand caught
in the door. The knee sliced nudging
a fish tank across the back seat of the car.

Beneath the curtain that last time, we watched
blood drop on the tiles and splash into smaller
drops. A man on the other bed had cut
his wrists, and we stopped the usual joking
and watched the black shoes of cops and the dropped
                gauze and the reflection
on the cabinet glass. He once had been
the luckiest man alive, he said.

Now you are in his bed. Teeth in the gauze. And I
on the metal stool, watch the stain soak from
the center, crust and hold a little till
it must be replaced.
Some boy has tracked your face. His cleats notched in
your chin, your lips, the bridge of your nose.

It is my last year for your emergencies.
You mumble, "Good."
Is there nothing more
to spare you? Scalpels or needles? Two dozen kinds
of thread, named and numbered in cardboard
boxes on the wall.
What will it be next year?
                          Rubble. The repeating sound
of fire. The dislocated bones.

   3

Last night in Esther's kitchen I saw
a photo from the *Times*. A Turkish woman in
Narman with five small sons laid out on the ground,
in the gentlest curve and her arms curved
above them, one elbow crooked just a bit, just so,
as she knelt on the stone.

And all the balance of the scene. And her mouth
open in communion with all dark
spaces.

If it had been art, someone would
have said: Too many. There should be just one or
two. Or someone would have thought the fractured earth
too obvious or uncontrolled.
But no one was there to sketch the scene for her.
And what did the woman know?

                                    The earth did
it. Cracked and toppled the village. And she laid out her
sons as best she could. Not knowing that
if she were an artist, she might
have saved most of them.

   4

A collagist once, I lacerated things.
Recombined and reinvented them. Set them off,
the visuals composed, the contents skewed.
Humor. Shock. Dispassion. The last laugh.
How young I was.
And how removed.

But somehow, inexplicable, from that fierce cutting
I saved those pictures, madonna and child, always
at the moment that is also pietà. When the lap
or ground has caught what is given, broken and taken
in the instant continuum that she knows the first
time the head wobbles on her arm.
The most classical and primitive of configurations:
the triangle of mother and child and what she broods.

Picture the head, small and abraded, pressed to the
olive sari that waits as it finishes its dying
on the road from what was East Pakistan. Or the
dehydrated flanks framed by the white cotton mantle
that falls from shoulders down the useless breasts in
the Sahel, in Upper Volta.
                              Or the hands that sponge
what they could not spare the deformed limbs
in Minimata, in Kyushu.
Even the girl at Kent State become
a mother to someone's crumpled son whose face
leans to the curb, away from what gave out
on the concrete drive.

                                                        33

I told Esther I could not take another picture.
Who can save any of them anymore?
This week a warehouse in Dover fills with wood from
Lebanon. Not cedar. It is pine wood. And boxes in bright
three-colored cloth come up from the beaches of Grenada,
come into the bass tones at the podium where the
air vibrates from hollow brass. Where a small triangle
is given. To be embraced to the breast. A folded flag.
Something to be saved.
We have sons that age, Esther said.
We know it would not be enough.

5

Who is she, the nurse asks.
Not even addressing me. I answer for you.
The cracked teeth and lip split clear, needing
no exegesis. Does she expect you to look down
and say in a calm and Galilean tone, "Behold."
   She scrutinizes me for rings, wrinkles,
growth signs. The old tree. Knobbed. Gnarled. Cut down.
At last I'll do.

At first she thought I was your lover.
And you, too tall to have this mother anymore.
Now the same vain flatteries we hear in
theaters and department stores. She leaves you
on the bed. Mud stripes your cheekbones, blackens out
your nose. You terrified a child as we passed through
the waiting room. Now it is bedtime and I am out
of stories.

         Who is she, I ask the cabinet
door. She was the green bell pepper
full of seeds, cut open on the board.
She was the dinghy-boat on whose
spine you rocked to shore. She was the vault

above the altar intoxicated by incense and
nonsense. Her ribs gone to rafters now like
the starved Buddha. She finds nothing left to give.

6

Now the quiet, light domestic scene. The blue-green
cloth unfolded, spread over your scalp, pulled down
across your forehead, eyes and nose.
A man is threading a needle and I
am asked to leave.
I, who have been there since
you were called down into existence.
I who was cast and drilled in the drama on
the square white stage whose yielding center
has pulled you and everyone into it.
Twenty I was. Too young for absolute expectancies.
I demanded nothing be given. But I did not know I would
be asked to go so soon.

Where is the plastic box, whose indented
gold letters say "teeth," where I keep
the four pulled out that summer in Stroudsburg,
still with their crooked undissolved roots.
Today it will have six. And it will not be enough.
Not ever enough. Not enough when Julia's sister
had her son back from Saigon. Only teeth.
She could see what they carried was
too light. What she had carried. And she could not
be deceived.

The doctor talks of college as he pulls.
Nine stitches. In the hall I count the sound of
scissor clips. Hear you mumble to his questions.
Incomprehensible. But more than you've given me today.
Once here, years ago, I asked you to be silent.
Were you so old even then, that you remember?

7

In the Grotte des Infants, among
the caves of Grimaldi,
were buried the bodies of son and mother.
Cro-Magnons. Now specimens. He, much taller,
kneels with his chin beside her ear. And
the beads that were his cap have fused to his
skull as the bones went bare. And see her hand
under his chin. Her other hand
with a bracelet of the same beads.
Head by head. Kneeling beneath her
where they have gone together.

Oh what would people say if they
were alive, or had a scrap of flesh left,
flesh that formed, separated, stank
and merged again.

8

On the wall the doctor shows the pictures.
Frontal. Parietal. Lateral. Occipital.
Life size. The grinning child.

The same grinning child who once
saluted his father's camera with a wave from
under water. The child
who posed in the ersatz classroom for
the fourth-grade photographer and smiled there
with the flag and autumn scene for his out-of-town
grandmothers. The child who stopped
midstep when the flashbulb went
in the living room where he danced with
the percussionist's deaf daughter.
                              The child
who dropped in the net and was preserved

in muck today for the high-school paper. A save.
Bloody and grinning. Still grinning.
                         No sign of
pain now in the two hollow orbits beneath
the fleshless tori, or along the sagittal suture
where the soft plates shut, where no dura mater,
no pia mater shows. No pain now
through the back, through the foramen magnum
where no mother should be asked to go, where I see
again the same dark opening I know, the gaping
space I thought I'd filled.

Whose Woods

mi ritrouvai per una selva oscura

I

Below his window
the doctor, old and self-indulgent, kept
his wolf pack.
The last known lobos. Untamable. Cannibal.
Adults paid a quarter
and children fifteen cents to see
them penned.

The first night in that bedroom
I couldn't sleep. I'd arrived too
late. There was no shade.
The moon was in some phase allowing
shadows of the closest
trees, though not the woods
a thousand miles square, sloping off
from where the pens had stood.

What had made me think they'd still
be there, though I'd pictured them rusting and
empty? Was it the photos at the nearby
school where the luncheon china
still bore those heads, canine to
an extreme, a few still unbroken.

All night the bedroom door stayed open.
It was fall and cold.
The registers downstairs, heat rose
when invited. And with it from
the mantel the imported clock
sent its disturbing tunes.

I watched the moon's slow arc. Conceived
how howls followed once an identical
progression. Through a dozen quarter chimes
I tossed. Then something forced
me down. It was at my ear,
my heels. I panicked, took the stairs, looked
for the unlocked door. But stopped
before the self-absorbed,
pale face, two metal
hands in a crystal case:
time's instrumental forgings whirred
and asked what thing I am.

Human was not the word that
came. It was
the other one, *mortal*: the thin
skin worn with the clock's permission.

Then, as if from some distance, I saw
my two hands
lift that clock.
I made them drop, withdrew my chance
to heave it off the porch and listen as its
glass and fluted columns
splintered off the trees where lobo whelps
were born each spring in metal cages and human
dominance.

II

Ron and Jessica live here on the edge,
containing the fire in this forest. Successors
to the doctor's hearth, she keeps
the files; he, the rifles.
Hers hold the wolves. His, lead and
brass: the forest keeps his casings.

Still gold as a girl's
her hair falls thick above her page, a gauntlet
flung at age, the challenge
yet untaken.
These nights, with the lamp pulled down
to her text, she retypes Shakespeare
through convex glass. By bed
an old scene's
been abridged for spring's indifferent class.

Still virginal, the forest shapes his
dream. His head propped by her embroideries,
he bends his knees up on the couch,
tallies his nightly figures, projects
a pension out against their budget and
the sum of all those trees he longs to
roam through in retirement.

From my chair cornered in the *L*-shaped
room, the files of clippings on my lap, I raise
my eyes from wolves and see them both,
a pair of time's persistent lovers
who cannot see each other.

Now to my left, the place mats shoved aside,
the swag illuminates her beauty,

pride and books: the burdens
I surmise he takes down to
those woods. Yet on my right he stretches out
in that exigent solitude that must
strike her like a disavowal
since she knows she cannot follow.

If I raveled out their thirty years of
trails zigzagging this wide Allegheny forest,
I'd see how unfailingly they revert
to their formative habitats:
to her father's wide estate above Lake Erie
where her bearing rose unchecked
in the clearing before the Depression;
or to his, the orphan home.

Now she commands the maple table.
He, the length of couch. Immobile. Seemingly
detached. Yet I see them hack their way
through my presumptions to meet, contented,
kinder than most, mated
for life out here, where I trespass
among trees ringed invisibly
with their endurance.

III

The headwaters of the Allegheny course
this forest. And its tributaries.
The Clarion. Tionesta. Kinzua.
And their tributaries. Salmon. Bear.
Big Mill. And Spring. Snow's melted
from the trails. The paved and
unpaved. Marked. And the unmarked.
The blazed, and the ones we
make ourselves. Believe me, there
are thousands.

Here and there a rusted derrick. Open wounds
time's refused to heal.
Indians knew this oil for their paints. And years
before the Declaration some whites took
it for their lamps, dosed themselves
for toothaches and rheumatism.
The woods are dark. Chilly. Damp.

Among the ruins, Jessica knows from
many years where there'll be salamanders:
I pierce the black, floating surface,
maple leaves on a transient pool.
My hand jumps from the cold. A mating pair
zigzag off in opposite directions.

Up near the dam, Cornplanter's grave.
There had been some outcry. Should
the bones be moved? Or the watercourse?
Now there's a clamor in the gorge:
the hidden peepers find some voice
a few spring evenings every year.

I read the speech Cornplanter made in Philadelphia.
A hard trek down from here, with the weight
of all his protests:
how the liquor had his people and the squatters
had his land. How his wife's brother
had been tomahawked by
a white man and dumped in one of these
rivers for his horse. How his nephew
had been ambushed, and his friend
shot in the back
as they crossed these woods
to Pittsburgh on another
try for justice.

By Philadelphia, it seemed so hopeless
he no longer called them *Brothers*.
Now it was *Fathers*.
He'd learned who owned the forest. The skins.
Canoes. Silver. Whatever modicum of value
his people toted on their deeded land.

Cornplanter's voice is gone now. And his
bones. A small degree of
wilderness. Only one
among the unselected species. A man
who believed that corn could save
his people in this maze. A man who ritually
buried his anger in the earth.

IV

There are tests out here. Runes to
be read. I will be led among trees, then left
with the brief instruction to go so deep I cannot
see the common redness of the house or hear
the cars coming from the knob factory
breaking at the sharp turn
in Tionesta Road.

Go down enough, there will be no smoke.
No sound from the half-tame dog who scents
an old encroachment
in his chains at the border cabin.
Go farther yet, where burrowing
ground squirrels reappear beyond
the range of house cats.

And there with shifting footing over past
years' leaves, see another
and another and another tree. Each one
living, organic as I am, even
producing what I breathe. But still
I can't settle in their maze, I resist
the connection, too skeletal and dark.
Go deeper yet. There are no marks.
No signs of destination.
And nothing
signals when to stop.

Light starts to fade in measurable
degrees: so here's the clock
where my mind once almost hurled it.
And now it's time
that must lead me back. Braking my pace
with its own unruffled plodding, leaving

me to shadows, or whatever is at hand.
It will make a path.
Always uphill.
Until the dog barks.

When I arrive, the typewriter has my place.
The cheddar's hardened on the maple board.
The fan's displaced the air above
the stove. I am changed.
And they know.
But it's not a thing to talk about.

After I've eaten, the keys click. And the usual
bell warns the endings of the lines.
To Ron I confess how one night
I nearly smashed that priceless clock. Years
have passed out here. But tonight I've finally
gotten used to time.
He shows a hinge. A hidden spring.
There's always a simple
lever to press to stop the tolling.

Now when he totes the rifle
down the ridge to stalk, I wait the hours
out with Jessica. Busying ourselves.
No need to talk. Now we both have seen
its tracks. That loneliness. Ferocious.
But then the redness of his cap.
The rifle on his shoulder. He hasn't
stopped it yet.

V

Ron and Jessica have gone west. His last
sabbatical. The Kane house closed, I cross
the woods, the failed attempts at
settlement: the untamable
scrub jungle northwest of Kane, the wild
untillable section west of Ludlow.
The forsaken gardens, the weedy
lots. The glacial boulders in what
was someone's house yard.

In Sheffield, Len and Kara have cleared a plot
and filled their roughed-out
shell. Already deer graze the garden.
Up in Warren, Kara starred in
Annie Get Your Gun. She warns
deerstalkers off her land, using good
manners when she can. Len keeps his
blackened boots in the garage.

Len totes a lunch pail to the motorworks.
But dinner's on Lenox. A matching set.
Unlike those hands that join above
the silver. I bow with grace and check
this mind that always has to speculate.

They tell about their wedding trip to
England. Her West End. Her hallowed
shrines. The softest beds his
engine and his maps could
find. We clean
our plates. Mate with mate. Hosts
with guest. Honoring our
contracts. Unlike the speculators who
first plotted out this place, and left a town
uncleared and unpaid for.

Out here in deeper woods, the nights are raw.
I sleep with Scott. Fat on rodents, and
warm. Zelda's gone, his mate, the shy one,
taken by the woods.
In time something seems to get
whatever's too domestic.

Was it only the sudden berserk heat of courtship
that sprung that grouse,
drumming through Kara's
tempered window?
Glass and feathers
on her Ethan Allen table.
Though no one speaks their language anymore,
Tionesta still means *home of the wolves.*

VI

In September, given up
on the abridgment of the *Tragedies*
Jessica types a letter: Something's
broken loose.
Not in the ways I had conceived. I had
seen the galleries of bark
beetles. The isolated frost-cracked
branches. Well shafts covered by rotted
boards, obscured by leaves. The crooked
holes, too dark to see what's
burrowed. Or buried. What could
get out. Inevitable
yet incidental casualties.

Instead it began with an unexplained low
roar, a sudden rain. The gutters clogged, Ron
crawled out on the roof, unscooped the maple seeds,
looked up and saw
the thick green cloud.

Out of breath,
from their basement they saw familiar
trees. The ones on Tionesta Road, nothing
like before, bent low, twisted themselves and
rose up dangling their roots.
Something howled.
Blew the windows from
the casings. Tore off a wall. Made
it easier to see the wood beside
the doctor's house:
A valley of stumps. Shards.
No trees.

Dispersed now, whittled away,
what once was leafed and whole.
Part of a vast tract that Cornplanter
sold for a hundred
mothy blankets and
a few commodities.
Then tired of all the contention he
deeded away his borders: left miles for
the wolf and fox. The bear and deer. A no man's
land left to
the pines and hemlocks.

Yet Jessica isn't moved to try
some neatly typed allusion to
a trespass over time.
She sticks to the facts. The more immediate
scene. Tonight she dismisses
history, the tale
told too often to signify.

She even passes up the irony of how the woods
have come against her
up the hill.
Something's left her unwilling to personify.
Or even to speculate what sort of thing
it was that came
and scattered who knows where
a stack of laundry from the table
where she and Ron had crouched.
Or what it was
that left the other stack
still folded.

Larkspur
for Sheila

Warm weather, and the couple who've moved in
across the street are raking. He wears a turban.
She a pair of jeans. I like their laughter
and their daughter, a small blond thing with
a dirty spoon, who on Sunday left larkspur
in my garden where they'll never grow.
She dismissed my talk on shade, said
she'll watch them from her window.
A flat, unstable star, her hand spread.
I obliged her. Tapped her packet till she'd
counted four and saw them: not hapless bits
of matter, but pink and purple as their picture,
the ribbings of her sweater. She broke
a clod. Dumped them. Tamped it with
a sneaker. Repeated her unsupported
hopes, and had me cross her.

On Saturday, among foiled mums, routine
baskets filled with leaves, a fake bird and one
true, tall spike of larkspur, I found my
son, stretched out with a girl, his
sleeve against her i.v. Thirty metal staples
marked the furrow. They took a kidney and
the thing it grew: Five pounds. Pink.
Ripe. And overdue. Some starry cells,
they say, are in there still.
So who's to pull this long boy from
her bed? A wise nurse. Or a mother.
This girl has neither. His dirty socks
accuse me of delinquencies. Of years when I
ignored their rumpled sheets, their washy
dreams, and waved them off to school. At noon
my husband crosses to the Rundel Library.
The texts abstruse, worded for doctors.
He phones me the statistics over lunch, varieties

that sound Linnean as the Burpee seeds we'd
meant to order. I too was twenty once.
They laid him on my chest. A five-pound bunch.
With no instructions, and little time to watch.

The Same Water

Sooner or later each kid who fishes
          in uneventful water
where the bob only bobs and is not pulled under
   will imagine the sameness of heaven
and by lunchtime will realize in his boredom
that all water converges
                   and must be shared by everyone.
He will see that his line extends thirty-six thousand
feet down into the Mariana Trench
                 and that in a hundred
million years, or maybe a lot sooner,
the waves licking his knees will slick the back
of a sixty-foot whale shark
            slumbering in an equatorial sea.
       It's a lure for any fisherman.

Even Jesus with his wet soles and
perfumed ankles wrapped in yellow hair, walking,
grew gradually aware how barnacles bleed the flesh and
         harrow our hulls.
He knew then, how few were saved.

Olav, my uncle, twice torpedoed and preserved,
   a merchant seaman who could tell you how to float,
would tell you how it's easier to go under.
       So much has gone under this July.

A fall has paralyzed a lifeguard
in the Town of Rye on Oakland Beach.
                Headfirst
off his watchtower.
         Eighteen, with a crushed vertebra.
And who is safe to swim now?

In Winona Lake, in Warsaw Indiana, even a magician's died.
He was handcuffed and chained and
               jumped in the water.

Twenty-three,
            and his magic failed him.
Yet all the water keeps converging,
demonstrably downstream,
                  or at least in the clouds.

When Carol, once my neighbor, came today for lunch
  she told how she still sees her father
                  padding clumsily
up the long pool outside their Cold Spring Harbor home,
under the watertight weight
                  of a brass helmet, trailing
an air pipe, a stream of small bubbles,
in twenty-pound boots, and eighty pounds of lead
belted at his waist.
                  And how his face in its clear, round
portal changed, blued and grimaced
while her legs dangled in the pool.
                        Nine years old
when he called to her with his hand
            slowly, repeatedly, through the water
to come and release the belt as he had shown her.
Frightened, she did not come.
And she did not leave him.

And it was the same water when my husband saw his
father in the morgue. Three months
  in the Harlem River, where it coves and the young
crews from Columbia pass, in their swift
sculls, the painted "C" on the bluff wall.
  The first day of spring,
                  his head crushed and some
of it gone.
We slept with a light till summer.

But still divers dream of finding only riches
in the wrecks off New Jersey where the surf
             can beat mean crazy,
off Ocean City where we all must go
to line the boardwalk and watch them go down
                                        and hopefully
come up
         with something.
Three thousand cases of Japanese curios
   lie in the *Sindia*'s hold.

And there or where you are, all the water's joining yet.
Ineluctable, even as we make for shore,
              it capsizes our pleasure boats, yields gory
stuff in the stomachs of tiger sharks, warps our
bindings, or wraps our London Fogs in odd, fishy smells,
              Year after year, it bobs our bobs
up to our knees
             in the same water.

The same water that brings whales back to Provincetown
   where tourists sing their "thar she blows."
And at the wheels, the scions of whalers
             pursue descendant whales,
   spot the spout, the fluke that bucks
                            and descends
before they can think too much
                      or follow.

Whales are not saddled with ghosts or animosity.

The tide reverses itself twice daily.

Some days the fishing is better.

Footprints grow fainter the farther away from the pool.

This summer Carol has moved to Long Point. The new
town houses off Ontario Street. "If it is time
for a change," the prospectus said.
                    And it is time.

Her wall of window faces the water.
The lighthouse with its round beacon, so close
                    she could toss a rope to it.
Or walk across the little inlet
to reach it, when it freezes.

My Father's Last Words
During the Breeders' Cup

I think I like Cruget on Palace Music in the mile
though Rousillon, the favorite, will be
hard to beat. And I won't care that it is
Guerra on Cozzene. Cruget will place,
and by the time he is disqualified for blocking
in the stretch, I will have died.
With the bed up now, I can make out the sign
over the OTB. Earlier I meant to send
the boy across. But, maybe it's late repentance,
I'll watch it uninvested on the screen, here in
intensive care, where the tv hovers like the Lord
and the numbers of my heartbeat flash in green.

So it's Pearson, dragging the curtain up the rod.
That means it's time. All wagers in. He's signaling
my wife and kids to leave. But I'll keep
my horses floating across the ceiling while I
sign some other paper I can't read.
He'll open up some vein. There'll be another tube.
I remember how Elaine's horse, bloated on apples, flew
across the field, the tubes they'd brought to
pump him, streaming from his nose.
All right. I'll go. Before the big race. Before
Piggot rides his last at Aqueduct today: half deaf,
he'll go direct, ignore their blame and praise.

Last night I saw they had a party for the Cup up at
the Museum of Natural History. The celebrities and owners
dressed in tuxes, and waltzed in the Hall of Ocean Life.
There was turf on the floor. Fences and a barn door.
And green felt covering the fish as if they
weren't there. So let it be green turf for me,
some small patch on this island I will share with
Belmont, Aqueduct and Roosevelt. But let it be out here
where the old potato farms are turned to paddocks
for the thoroughbreds. And before I rest my head let

Bill Tarpey drive from West Point to say how fast I was,
how crowds coming from Yankee games would stand
at Macombs Dam Field to watch me throw, and let his
brother Marty remind them, too, how I raced
under the Harlem River, farther than anyone could go.
Then let my wife be proud. She who took me with
my gambling debts, who saw me gamble here and lose,
let her count a hundred wreaths of flowers.

About the author

Joan Murray grew up in New York City, and the iconography of
South Bronx buildings and Harlem River bridges is a presence in
her poems, along with features of the shore and woodland com-
munities where she has lived and worked. She was educated at
Hunter College and New York University and has taught literature
and writing at Lehman College of the City University of New York.

She has won several awards for her poetry, including a 1989
National Endowment for the Arts Grant, a 1988 New York Foun-
dation for the Arts Fellowship, two New York State Council on
the Arts Grants, and a Pushcart Prize. Murray is an instructor in
poetry for the New York State Literary Center, a consultant for
the New York Foundation for the Arts, and an arts lobbyist rep-
resenting the statewide constituency of individual artists for the
New York State Arts and Cultural Coalition. She is at work on
a novel and a booklength poem. She lives in upstate New York.

About the book

This book was composed on a Compugraphic MCS digital type-
setting system in Galliard, a contemporary rendering of a classic
typeface prepared in 1978 by the British type designer Matthew
Carter. The book was composed by Lithocraft of Grundy Center,
Iowa, and designed and produced by Kachergis Book Design of
Pittsboro, North Carolina.